Riding the Wave Train

poems
RHONDA
PETTIT

DOS MADRES

2017

DOS MADRES PRESS INC.
P.O.Box 294, Loveland, Ohio 45140
www.dosmadres.com   editor@dosmadres.com

Dos Madres is dedicated to the belief that the small press is essential
to the vitality of contemporary literature as a carrier of the new voice,
as well as the older, sometimes forgotten voices of the past. And in an
ever more virtual world, to the creation of fine books pleasing to the
eye and hand.

Dos Madres is named in honor of Vera Murphy and Libbie Hughes,
the "Dos Madres" whose contributions have made this press possible.

Dos Madres Press, Inc. is an Ohio Not For Profit Corporation and a
501 (c) (3) qualified public charity. Contributions are tax deductible.

Executive Editor: Robert J. Murphy

Illustration & Book Design: Elizabeth H. Murphy
www.illusionstudios.net

Typset in Adobe Garamond Pro & Cracked
ISBN 978-1-939929-80-8
Library of Congress Control Number: 2017943427

First Edition

ACKNOWLEDGMENTS

I gratefully acknowledge the following publications in which my work or earlier versions of it first appeared:

Journals
Colere, "Aubade"
Drash: Mosaic Northwest, "Meditation at Useless Bay"
For a Better World 2017, "The Gift Child"
Freedom Center Journal, "Eve Gathering Apples"
Journal of Kentucky Studies, "The Postmistress," "This Light This
    Time," "Mermaids at Midnight," "Super Model," "Mother
    the Stranger"
Licking River Review, "After the D&C"
New Hampshire Review, "The Mermaid Parade"
Pine Mountain Sand & Gravel, "Red Lace"
Seneca Review, "Cirrus"
Sugar Mule, "Something about Us"
The Raven Chronicles, "The Harvesters"
The Single Hound, "1963"
Tipton Poetry Journal, "Epistemology"
Xanadu, "The Transposition Blues"

Anthologies
*I Go to the Ruined Place: Contemporary Poems in Defense of
Global Human Rights*, "Enfant Terrible"
Quarried: Three Decades of Pine Mountain Sand & Gravel, rpt.
    "Red Lace"
Raising Lilly Ledbetter: Women Poets Occupy the Workspace,
    "Assessademia"

Some of these poems, or earlier versions of these poems, appeared in my chapbook *Fetal Waters*, published by Finishing Line Press, 2012, or in my Cincinnati Fringe Festival production of *The Global Lovers*, 2010.

Thank you to the funding sources and writing retreats that have contributed to my efforts over the years: Kentucky Arts Council, Kentucky Foundation for Women, Virginia Center for the Creative Arts, Hopscotch House, Hedgebrook Retreat for Women, Hambidge Center for Creative Arts & Sciences, writing retreats at Sisters of Loretto Motherhouse in Nerinx, KY, Southern Appalachian Writers Cooperative, and the Community of Writers Retreat Series at the Thomas More College Biology Field Station. A special thanks to the University of Cincinnati Blue Ash College and its Department of English and Communication for granting academic leaves during which much of this work was produced. A belated thanks to James Baker Hall (1935-2009) whose teaching and dedication to the art of writing remains a guiding light for many.

To Michael Lee Horn

wave train (wāv trān) n. a succession of waves occurring at periodic intervals and traveling in the same direction, esp. a group of waves of limited duration.

"It is a confused pattern that the waves make in the open sea—a mixture of countless different wave trains, intermingling, overtaking, passing, or sometimes engulfing one another; each group differing from the others in the place and manner of its origin, in its speed, its direction of movement; some doomed never to reach any shore, others destined to roll across half an ocean before they dissolve in thunder on a distant beach."
— Rachel Carson, *The Sea Around Us*

"The sea has many voices . . . hollow boomings and heavy roarings, great watery tumblings and tramplings, long hissing seethes, sharp rifle-shot reports, splashes, whispers, the grinding undertone of stones, and sometimes the vocal sounds that might be the half-heard talk of people in the sea . . . . [I]t is also constantly changing its tempo, its pitch, its accent, and its rhythm . . ."
— Henry Beston, *The Outermost House*

"It is always the unseen that most deeply stirs our imagination, and so it is with waves."
— Rachel Carson, *The Sea Around Us*

TABLE OF CONTENTS

Prologue

I. *. . . after becoming, waves may travel . . .*

II. *. . . the very father of all waves . . .*

III. *. . . only the wave form moves.*

IV. *The greater the fetch, the higher the waves.*

V. *A second sea rises . . . .*

Epilogue

Prologue

THIS BREATHING ROCK

One lived as long as one could, living
among a cluster of others living as long
as they could, secreting their shells,
opening to feed, closing to protect, eventually
pried open or drilled through and devoured,
or frozen by cooler water or left parched
by retreating seas, a residence that had changed
its mind, a mind that was larger, vaster
than any one shell could hold, distant
and recalcitrant, calculating and disinterested,
downright aggravating: radiating abundance
then extinguishing the light on one side
of the bed. Who or what would find them
again, not just the what of what remained
of life, but evidence of the turbulence,
the hurricane, the furnace, the freeze-
thaw cycle? How would that book, that story,
that song tell the seekers, the accidental finders-
keepers what to do, think, worship
regards this breathing rock with its
living sands in the hands of deep time?
Waves of laughter, waves of woe. Pauses,
scratches, impressions of an old record
turning. *Aggravatin' poppa, don't you try
to two-time me,* wails Bessie Smith tonight.

I.

. . . after becoming,
waves may travel . . . .

1963

Eight years old
and living in Kentucky,
what did I know

about the Negro boy
who watched from the other side
of the swimming pool fence?

Arms above his head,
he clutched the hot chain links
topped with barbed wire,

his striped shirt high above his navel.
Did he see the water or the metal?
What did I know?

He was damp with sweat.
He was not allowed in.
He was my age.

He disappeared when someone's father
or the lifeguard said: *Go on
now, get home!*

What did I know?

Chlorine and Coppertone, the sun
glaring from water and concrete,
blinding us all.

CHANGELING, 1964

The crack of a bullwhip makes a small
sonic boom, makes large animals obey,
and scars and stripes forever human flesh,
but I didn't yet know such things.
I was standing by the garage door
the instant the invisible supersonic
aircraft boom-shattered the air around
me, violating the boundary between me/not
me, as if now I would hold my breath
for years without knowing it, always be
dying to keep a step away from death.
It pounded the walls and windows, the bass
of it a god gone devilish with invention,
the meaning and meanness of its music
a suddenly familiar tremor in my bones:
the earth was being remade and I
was less than nine, less than small,
less than a name, less than now.
I was the grand-daddy long-legs thrown
hard against the garage door today,
and I was the hand that threw it.

OCEAN DIORAMA, 1965

I walk with my family along the narrow platform
peering through thick round glass
and see bottom, and see all
below us is not hell.

Aside from the ship's hull,
the picket fence of pirate bones,
the fallen, empty chest,
Paradise remains:

forever pink anemone cluster in sand,
yellow sea lilies arch in mid-bob,
lamp shells glisten above green
brains of coral
sharing their beds with stars;

and there
among tentacles everywhere on the verge and
white fish groping near orange sponges,
among fans and beads and whips,
the mannequin mermaids
pose in blue light.

Two of them lounge in oysters;
their queen in the middle claims the anchor,
fins curled like hands released
from prayer.

Somewhere a mirror reveals
our faces, and a voice free
from the garble of water
finds us:

Hey Doll,
it says to my father,
How'd ya get so handsome?
Where y'all from? Why don't cha come and
take a swim?

It listens, it lures, it praises Florida waters,
and turns to me – *Where'd ya get those pigtails?* –
after he turns away.

I take this vision
into the rest of Webb City,
down aisles of swimwear and sporting goods,
toys and cosmetics, through the stale scent
of straw hats and popcorn.

I take it home.
Did it not take me as well
into its sculpted hair and dripless painted faces,
into its room of dry tides
where anything but love is blue

light, and once a week
the sea needs dusting?

BAPTISM

I knew I was supposed to believe
in something, but what other than
the wetness ascending my legs?
That the minister's grip could be
trusted? That salvation would not
have its sting? *Close your eyes,*
he whispered, tilting me back and down,
but I left them open to see the face
of God. It blurred into anger and
absence as I rose, a wave crashing
on a shore of air, the congregation
mute and obedient as angels. None
of them smiled. Now I was one
of them, committed to possession,
to keeping belief and certainty,
to washing away the difference between
the two, to disregarding the old saw:
Don't drink where you bathe.

Born Again

Small breasts emerged like thorns
just before my first period came,
more of a tea stain than a bounty
rejected that made me feel a wisdom
I didn't understand and wasn't sure
I wanted, but there it sat on the porch
like an invisible Goodyear blimp between
Terry Blood (of all names to have at my
grand opening!) and me, the quiet of it
transposing to a contract
neither of us had signed. All we did
was talk but Terry was smiling when he
jumped off the porch and ran home, as if
I had made him feel a wisdom, too.
Was this power? What was I
supposed to do with it? The next few months
would answer, doubling me over with cramps,
Midol, and dry heaves as if my uterus
had a mind of its own, angry at the waste
to be. When would I know my new body
the way I had known the now fossil
of my young one? When could I trust it,
like it again? *It's called your Possible,*
my grandmother had told me before the blood,
naming the deep south of our bodies
while we stood at the kitchen window
washing dishes, watching a Southern Railroad
freight train rumble-rush across the trestle,
a long, noisy sentence finally punctuated
by a red caboose. The rattle of its north-bound journey
echoed back to us. My grandmother broke
like glass the silence that had shelved us

for the moment to repeat: *Your Possible.* All
this was long before I had looked down,
accidently found the first red curl of pubic hair, a lone comma
on the low slope of my belly, as if it were waiting,
waiting, waiting for the words for *what next.*

Swim Club Girl

When I swam in the whites-
only pool near the top of the hill,
its fencing crowned
with barbed wire,

its water enclosed by concrete,
I didn't think
of myself as
a prisoner,

but as a porpoise, a mermaid,
a body in water, a body of water.
I coursed its clear ocean until
cramped toes
took my breath away
and I flopped on dry land,
human again,

Cloud Nine, Tears of a Clown,
Rainy Night in Georgia
on the radio,

eyes squinting with sun
and sting. Where was my towel
and the lotion for my pale legs?
Now that I was out, I wanted
dark skin without the burn.

History Lesson

I.
I am listening to Grandmother Grace
in the paneled dining room, remnants
of repast and the past between us.

Three-hundred acres your Great-great-great
Pappy Logan owned, and slaves near Leesburg.
They say he was good to them, freed them
after the war, didn't want to leave. Sons
drank and gambled the farm away.

                                    What to say now?
I stare through the eyes of the knotty pine.
Behind them, a brick wall.

II.
Grace raised a Southern Baptist.
Grace with no father by twelve.
Grace who desired to believe.
Grace raised to love and obey.
Grace with the need to stay safe.
Grace who desired to believe.
Grace raised to cause no harm.
Grace with old stories to tell.
Grace who desired to believe.

III.
Grace raised.
Grace with.
Grace who.

Grace when.

II.

. . . the very father of all waves . . .

MIDNIGHT AT THE FOSSIL MOTEL

I.
1954-55

In her time before mind, when she
was a creature of water, a cord away
from earth; when survival was fluid
and knowledge a space without words, she
siphoned the pulse, hunger the little malignancy
that grew her into being, her growing the lesson
in restlessness, in knowing time. When at last
she broke through the first sea, entered
the world owning her own emptiness,

she howled to be filled, to keep going
on this breathing rock.

II.
1966-67

Her father, in the basement, calls to her:
I'm going to quit smoking before it kills me.
She looks down from the top of the stairs,
TV light behind him, twelve steps between them.
Now, at eleven, and for the length of his sentence
and her reply, she is his equal, an adult.
They've reached an agreement: an extinction
will occur, their world made free from its past,
their lives no longer etched in stone.

*

One of the Lucas girls points to a rock
and says, *Look – a fossil,* and tells her what
that is while they stand in the woods between
the cul-de-sac they live in and the high school
baseball field, one a circle with one way in and out,
the other a boys-only cone that opens to infinity.
In the late spring quiet of late afternoon, fathers not
yet home: crack of wood on a curve ball, dust
rising from the infield.

*

Sixth grade, after school, in the old house known
as the public library, she parks herself
on a wooden chair with an old *National Geographic,*
the only way she knows to go to Africa, to crawl
on her hands and knees with the Louis B. Leakeys.
Or to scour the Mobi with Roy Chapman Andrews.
Or to find in her mind the little proofs
of having been   becoming what   resistant
and whispering: *This . . . you are part of This . . .*

The neighborhood kids go to Catholic school.
Their Mary, rippled in blue and white stone,
looks down from a pedestal with delicate hands
and a chiseled smile for cherubs of sin.
Her Mary, under an old straw hat, crawls
on her hands and knees, nose to the stone
for Olduvai tooth, jaw, or bone, tracking
the black of our origins. They seek their Mary.
Her Mary seeks, finds the old toolmaker.

*

Lion's Park in winter is a raw plateau,
sheared of grass from summer fairs, wind, and rain.
She stoops there as her father watches, wishes
he had his Winstons. She will by god find
an Ordovician fossil. She will put her hands
on the mystery, the hard and fragile life long
gone and back again, breathless, blue in the shale
of a second sea. She walks with her eyes, pausing to name,
her torso a delicate comma she will have to undo.

Down slope, the interstate traffic howls.

*

Eden here is near the bottom
of the chart she copied for her wall
that lists the eras and periods of time
in which her fossils lived and died. Eden here
is older than the Bible, older than anyone's
early man. Eden here is mud and ooze,
saving the lace of ancient life, crushed
by time into singing the blues. Exposed
as shale and revelation.

*

Here is an odd piece, a bumpy something
on a flat shell half-buried in limestone.
From under dry waters under earth
she sets it down, her magnifying lens
a wavering layer she steadies between her eyes
and identity: an ancient sea urchin
attached to the shell like a cyst,
harmless to its host, and rare. Not
every find is a keeper. This is.

III.
SPRING-SUMMER, 1968

In the basement she holds her latest
fossil finds, this one the mold of a clam,
that one the whorl of a snail. A pan of hot water
soaks the others   *what what what will the water reveal?*
          loosening soil, releasing
the shaley-blue dank of sun-baked clay,
earth steam a whiff shy of fecal.
She has dipped her hands in the water
and the waterborne clay clings again,
scenting her, claiming her for its own.

She breathes it in, feels at home there.

*

Upstairs the peal of stainless steel pots,
her mother washing dishes, wishing her daughter would dry
but letting it go. Instead she stares out the window,
night blank as a future for all her watching.
What, other than the patio cracked in two?
The gentle slope beside the house, the gravity
of rain-swollen clay sliding down, pushing up,
drying out, dropping down again. Years of this.
She can't see past it. Love stops nothing.

*

Downstairs her daughter turns up the radio,
turns a page in her guidebook   *what what what?*
reads the pictures: she is still on the slope
of the roadcut, searching for patterns that say
to her *life*, for knobs and rings, ribs and cells,
lines that repeat like a song. In her hands
the thing and the scent of the thing,
no walls between earth and home,
page and stone, fossil and now.

*

Upstairs her father clears his throat,
tries again. The newspaper winces aloud
as he turns and folds it, props it for light
and distance. *Can Nixon end this damn war
or not,* he thinks. *My son, my son. Why won't
my fingers heal? Where is honor? My wife
and daughter. Fair, what's fair? Still burns when I piss.
This house. My business. Will there be enough money?
Enough time?* He clears his throat again.

*

Downstairs his daughter is running into time.
The object matching picture has to stand
by words and strata. The brilliant ones,
now scrubbed and dried, are numbered
and assigned their names, then put
to their new beds: clear plastic boxes
sectioned and lined with cotton. Her lab
a motel of stone, of the breathing rock
that rises, falls, rises in her chest.

*

Upstairs their footsteps, their voices, the words
too caked in matrix to be found. They are
coming down: nine o'clock and the lab is closed,
the TV on, science replaced by *Bonanza*.
She takes her fossil books upstairs,
thumbs, reads, dreams. Then and now.
She lives in both, but given a choice,
she'll take a dry sea, the burnt crust of time
over now's filling. The search. No walls.

IV.
FALL, 1968

Fossil. She loves the word in her mouth,
on her tongue, how you can't say *fossil*
without its whisper in the middle, the small
moan of its closing, its meaning's lack of closure,
the quiet it leaves behind as it disappears,
a sound for stone not caught in stone,
a breath, a gap, a god. Gone.
Unlike *loss,* which never stops whispering.
Unlike *found*: in-hand, here, but what?

*

How many times did she falsely name?
How many times did desire let her see
what was not to be found, let her skip
a fine point or a telling line, possession
confused with clarity? How many times did she
hold to the surface, keep to the top of the slope?
Why did the fossil in-hand feel true,
answer to any name she used, beckon her
in dreams, hold her like a lover? Let go?

*

Tumor (the word enters her as words usually do,
but refuses to float, disperse, disappear. It drops
from a height she didn't know she had, a boulder
knocking, nicking, chipping off bits of her she didn't know
she had that fell like gravel: landing, collecting,
reaching the well-spring she didn't know she was,
blocking it, more of her gone than she knew),
her mother said at the kitchen table,
Your father has a tumor.

24

*

As if the compulsions that made and remade this;
as if the blind luck that let it survive the earth's
acidic and twisting appetites, then exposed it
and brought her to the road-cut; as if
when finally she holds this she could be
earth   keeping it   absorbing it   resisting   if only
holding could stop   love could stop   keep the forces in-hand.
She reaches down, cars passing behind her.
Where are they going   where can she go

*

Daughter element, after all, long a part of her
vocabulary, the science that said her childhood god
held life in a hand much older than believed,
tossed it like dice after all; the science that said
he left it in the layered dark to fend for itself
or be lost and found by chance and circumstance,
must not have loved it enough, must not have
loved it like she did, letting it disappear
after all,   a Father   who art   unstable

*

As if the mystery itself, the secret she desires,
the cosmic gossip she would settle for,
the unshared thing were as hard
and finite as the object that keeps it,
as the fossil. As if it could be found
in the word she knows for the object itself,
in the infinite hush between *s* and *s*,
in the emptiness of the *o* of love, loss,
fossil. Anytime. Anywhere. Anyone's *o*.

V.
WINTER, 1972

This is not the death she seeks, reads about, knows, collects.

This is not the death she wants to scrub, name, keep with the
    others in a box
        of compartments, take out and hold, magnify and
            watch under bright light.

These are not the ulcerated hands with hammer and chisel that
    helped her chip chip
        chip the life out of limestone.

This is not the voice of *Yes   No   Sing a song of sixpence*
    It's time to wake up
        You are my sunshine, my only sunshine . . .

Cries, flailing, garbled words: this is not the music.

Mud-green bile and gurgling: this is not the loose soil on the
    matrix that shadows
        the *what what what* the water reveals.

This is not the thing love made. That spoke to her.

This is not the breathing rock.

This is not in-hand.

VI.
DREAMING OUT OF DEEP TIME

i.

She quits collecting
         what is missing
her dreams evolve
         who can tell
fossils emerge
         rooms for the transient
earth like a hand
         offering her
luck that looking
         sometimes made
she can't believe
         no dream this time
holds in her hands
         find of a life
love is a reckoning
         she is a part of this
what what what
         howl on the highway
where can she go
         what a dream knows
she disappears
         still she remains
weathered to pieces
         layer by layer
collected by someone
         peers from above
heart of the thing
         where   where
what is missing
         someone's awe

held and loved
                imagined and named
shelved
                like she did
dissolution
                like she was
of soft parts
                makes hard
what what what
                this case

    ii.

The Fossil Motel
                Open at midnight!
No reservations needed!
                Always a vacancy!
Give your dreams a rest!
                Sleep like an eon:
Benthic sleep systems
                blue Edenic linens
trilobite pillows!
                Shingled beds available!
(pedicles not included)
                No walls! No rooms!
No boxes! No names!
                Nothing but the hush
between *s* and *s*!
                Rattled or scattered sleep
relatively undisturbed!
                Residence without place!
Resonance in place!
                We accept I.O.U.!
Ask about our old
                unconformity rates!

The Fossil Motel bids you:
        Come in from the hurricane!
Join the Ordovician Radiation!
        Welcome to all
perilous gills and salt-driven hearts,
        creatures secreting,
opening, siphoning!
        Bankrupt shells and weary rocks!
Molts, molds, and mineral stains!
        Metaphors on the half-shell
hardening into curves!
        Floaters and parasites,
whatever you are!
        Even the poets may
come to compose
        their couplets of limestone and shale!
Seek and ye shall find
        departure's line of hardware
the writing beyond
        the wall:

Clean and tidy, open and spacious.
Nestled in the middle of nowhere.
Amenities functional, bed was firm.
Not sure we'll be back.

Original parts can disappear,
        original colors are rare,
but all come back
        and leave an impression
for luck, for love,
        for how long
who can say
        what is missing

iii.

what what what
is this part
of you what
this is part
of is what
you are part
of is part
of what this
is a part
of yes what
is this all
of you this
is yes all
of us here
in the hush
between *s*
and *s* is

a second sea rising

over this breathing rock

VII.
NOW AND THEN

She revisits the book she had always reached
for first, the thin paperback, its blue cover
softened and fuzzed like a miser in love;
tanned and loose at the binding; stained
inside and out by water and mud,
the occasional crumb of dissolving shale,
the red specks from a split cuticle.
This the book that name by name,
plate by plate, had defined the many lives

that filled her like a song's endearing
woe. Old now, her fossil book nearly
a fossil itself, some of its names never meant
to last. In part, a history of error, a chance
to learn from mistakes. She holds it
in-hand, the old loves returning – timeless, shell-less
floaters in the gene pool that had made
their long way to her making, beautiful
in the abstract, brutal in the abiding:

gray and weathered free.

*

Her collecting evolves. What she finds
she carries in her empty hands, a risk.
What were the odds? Rising from a bit
of fossil shell was a thin fan of bryozoan,
a small wave frozen in stone,
a contour of blind trust. It had survived
all the slap-dash love, the twist and contortion
the earth had to give, had found and collected her.
What are the odds? Everything to one.

III.

. . . only the wave form moves.

EPISTEMOLOGY

Knowing comes like an old man,
slowly, taking the flat road around,
too weak in the knees
to walk over stones,

damn sure of itself when it gets here.
It complains of all the bother,
teeth yellowed, face bristled
with reason.

What have you got now,
it asks, slumping into the rocker,
taking its aspirin with rye.
You thought it might

give comfort. Instead,
you'll have to help it eat and bathe,
listen to it snore, be there
if it wakes.

Aubade

—*for Michael*

Head heavy
with last night's Cotes du Rhone,
I rise around six and sit
on our balcony while
you sleep. One by one

the cafes circling
Place Voltaire release
themselves: security gates lift
like silver suns amid
gear-song, locks unclick,

long chains
unrattle tables and chairs
and peal into plastic pails,
mops shush and drown
assorted dirts,

streets shot
arrows of gutter froth. Then silence,
sure as a swallow of wine,
intoxicates the air,
enfolds all save

the occasional puff
of your breathing. All along
an old man bundled
in flesh and wool
has sat outside

Le Narval Café,
smoking his pipe and scratching
a dog's back. If he stays
I'll come back to bed.
If he leaves

I'll follow him
down a narrow street.
Look for us along the Rhone
singing, though I don't
know French.

THE HARVESTERS

The crop was in, our kitchen
was bursting to August with basil,
a scent as good as sex, or nearly so,
and we were minting our annual
feast of green: pesto to keep us
summering through fall
and winter.

The TV played *Who's Killing the Great Chefs of Europe?*
while I plucked and cleaned each leaf before
the simple palette of pungencies:

the gold and creams
of olive oil, garlic, parmesan, pignoli,
all to be subsumed by our backyard version
of Italy's kiss-me-Nicholas,

each one into the Other, the only path
we take in any kind of garden,
the joy before the joining
what we make.

It was a party of two
until we saw, on the soffit above us,
a young praying mantis, half a shade
lighter than the basil it rode
to our making,

and hungry, no doubt, for its camouflage,
the sumptuous menu promised by seduction.

We caught it in a plastic bowl,
set it outside among sage and avocado,
hibiscus and lavender, said our goodbyes.
What felt like a blessing was pure
accident, which only made us
hungry for more.

AFTER THE D AND C

—for Jay and Lorain

This morning a doctor will scrape
a tiny piece of you onto a glass slide,
and look at you through a lens,
and what might have been your face,
your hand, your brain, or the place
where your heart stopped beating
will look back, and likely as not,
refuse to tell your story. Stubborn
little muse, why did you say no?
Two people loved you enough
to say yes, and for nine weeks
you concurred. Now you are less
than a statistic, less than
the sugar and protein that ribboned
you into the womb. We are left
to make peace with that, to walk
away from the book just started,
the plot that brings us down to life,
as easily carried on as interrupted
by mysteries we haven't learned to read.

CIRRUS

Even your name is a whisper
your lightness less

than a feather
a flightness of water

a frond of weather
a wisp of gathering to come

snips from a pale spool
a silver stitch

lisp of a faint direction
a whim, a wink

a willowing hush
buss on a blue cheek

Suite for Opal

KEY SIGNATURES

My mother's mind is an old score
aged further by dementia

and yet is coyly modern
with its music, its notes escaping
their bars, replaced with increasing
frequency by silence
or the *eh* of a low-
register E.

These days I am neither
her daughter nor the mother
she calls in her song.

I am the novice musician
learning to read her grand staff
and locate the key

of her evolving composition –
how many sharps,
how many flats –

listening to feel the tempo
of each day's measure.

Time is different, she says.
Sometimes it jumps.
Sometimes it stops.

THE ALZHEIMER'S WING

is called The Arbor
as if a metaphor for natural seclusion
could make organic its padlocks
and keypads;

as if flight
from among the hollows and limbs
and crayoned leaves meant
choosing to go;

as if it held nests
of beginnings its peeping inhabitants
could grasp again;

as if it were the poem
we read in high school and failed
to understand

because it was difficult,
full of strange lives full of blanks

and stranger words,
making us mad

with distance.

SUNDOWNING

On a hill in southern Newport,
in the third-floor parlor of the nursing home,
we sit at dusk before a wall of windows,
portal and shield, a hologram dancing

while we remain.
I watch a blood of colors rise from pollution
and fade; neon scores the dark valley
as houses blink into stardom
and guide us to the river.

What does she, a gathering darkness,
see from the hold of her wheelchair?

     window   *a mother thing*   *a space,*

she says, arms and body reaching forward,
vinyl and metal stuttering the song
of her shifting weight.

   John, she says,
a name not my father's,
her eyes in love with the invisible.
She is outside of time and somewhere
between herself

and the glass

where memory and dementia unfurl
their ribboned gift: a world that accepts her

briefly on her own terms, the scene
beyond it mere drapery,
and beside her

I am the forgotten
who wheels her back and forth in space.

I am the missing,
the god without the word,
unable to enter her moment
of pure creation.

CONVERSE

(converse derives from old French and Latin words meaning:
to live with)

Gradually
I ceased talking to my mother
and began to address her dementia:

How are you doing?
Did you eat your lunch?
Would you like to take a walk?

At first it replied
like a curious child, wide-eyed,
with nods and smiles,

or determined to meet me half-way,
would answer *yes yes yes.*

In adolescence it grunted resentments—
        Jesus isn't nice to me
                I'm lost in time—
as if I had never given it toys to lose or break,
or kept it safe for its own good.

Then it grew up and grew
distant with fatigue from its company of strangers—
        my mother, my brother, and me—
the constant work we required, and none of us
saying thank-you.

Who can blame it
for leaving us today without a word,
taking everything we thought
was ours?

SHORTHAND

". . . training my hand to keep up with my brain."
-—Effie B. Smither, *Gregg Medical Shorthand Manual,*
1927, 1942.

Her manicured fingertips used to be
red bullets rifling through show tunes,
but she traded her Baldwin for an Underwood,
her music scholarship
for secretarial school.

Now there is rust on the corner
of the page in her shorthand manual,
paper-clipped nearly sixty years ago,
two words

and their venous script underscored:
pericardial, pericardium,
sac that holds the human
heart and root

of our vascular system.

Symbol for symbol,
one more level of language away
from experience, shorthand committed her
to memory and practice, to know so well its execution
would be as thoughtless as her old songs.

I never thought to ask her
why those two words,

but the shorthand for *dementia,*
not underscored or starred in the black
ink of her fountain pen,
resembles a wave
crashing

over rock.

MERMAIDS AT MIDNIGHT

We swam first,
naked as old shells
the tides scrub to shore,
then lay high among buried nuns,
watched stars in their decline and felt
the August air press us,
heavy as dirt.

We'd all had trouble
with love – husbands and children
continents away from our writing retreat,
or the thing itself so deeply layered and molten
we only knew it through
eruption, the odd fissure
an eon would close.

So we laughed
about the night watchman
who had peeked through the pool fence
and said, *Ladies, let me know if you need
any help.* We'd saved ourselves
with water, darkness,
and the muted

pool house light
that blurred the lines, the lacks,
the excess of our middle-aged bodies now
drying on the cemetery concrete. We laughed
at the shade between death
and desire, knowing how
it shaped us.

IV.

The greater the fetch,
the higher the waves.

Something about us

In the wedge of mown grass
between interstate ramps
along the old but busy highway,
a lone plant of Queen Anne's Lace
asserts, for now a white vehicle
of stillness. How many thousands
driving by to somewhere today
will notice this, take this, keep this
in their mind's vase?

How did it survive the blade,
or did the mower loop around it
nearly grinning? Or is it the first
to return, uncowed, inspired by the violence
used to tidy the land? It knows
something about us.

Invader from the Old World,
food for the brooding Black Swallowtail,
source of our domesticated carrot,
summer lover of wasted fields –
and it stinks, too. Anything this
accomplished sings of weed.

Here amid crossroads above
and below, amid concrete and asphalt, steel
and carbon monoxide, with all necessary
betrayals to the contrary, its tiny
clustered blossoms open
my window

where looking out
is looking in.

MOTHER THE STRANGER

my heart is open country now
low sky on a flat plain

a lone horse splits its hoof
on a stone
                hobbles off

*

mountains holding down
the horizon, blocking weather

all that comes down this side
image of rain
                we won't feel

*

bloody light in the canyon
the last fist unfurls

if no one remains to grasp,
pull it up,
                what good that prayer

*

red valves pumping, urging
to be no stranger

if I bear my heart as my nation
how is love made
                without weapons

*

not a machine, but machine-like
not a lone horse

but who would trade that split hoof
for bit, reins, the hand
                    behind them

*

once I loved a rancher
who left the ranch for the city

who left the city for war
whose bones make soil
                    for the desert

*

us / them: a history
without names

a storm without cease
without rain
                    in the heartland

*

script on the stone that split
the hoof: *mother the stranger*

noun or verb, I ask
says a lone horse,
                    both

55

INSTRUMENTS OF WAR

The guitar in the newspaper photograph
seems stranded, lying on the ground
instead of in someone's arms, and so
its music cannot be imagined.
Perhaps that is why it caught
my eye first, then let it go

to wander from body to body
up the long ravine, soldiers splayed out
like the ribs of some giant, fossilized beast
we like to think has disappeared.

Which one of the dead
was the soldier troubadour
who might have sung of love and beauty
and justice, all the same note? How many
had he killed in spite of this
before an ambush found
him off-beat?

The men and their war are history,
the photograph is evidence,
and the guitar,
like the gun,

fell from the soldier's hands
when hands and minds failed him
for the last time.

The instrument seems to survive –
no bullet holes, no broken neck,
all strings attached – survives in the silence
of an image.

THE TRANSPOSITION BLUES
(C to E, with dynamics)

Key of C   Key of E

Pianíssimo

Sea anemones   Image to quench
puckering near the neap tide stones.   whose thirst for torture?

Mézzo Piano

Bird song   Caged birds
deep from the belly of the hawk.   released for the hunt.

Con Timidezza

In winter the sun   Cocoon of words
rising behind clouds.   where no peace is made.

Legato

A wishbone of limb   The child who lost
lodged in the wind-driven maple.   an arm carries a rifle.

Crescéndo

The tulip pink between   Raised to obey authority
boulders reluctant to open.   she bludgeoned the difference.

Fortíssimo

An elderly woman   Moment that signals
sasses the sleepless night.   a nation in menopause.

Staccáto

At the storm's fringe,
concrete spittled by rain.

Beware the beloved land
made holy by rote.

A Dúe Córde, Poco Adagio

How the couple calls
their love: deeply igneous.

This goat and sack of grain
for a twelve-year-old wife.

A Témpo Rubáto

Trying to touch love,
and not just the body, she . . . .

When nothing could stop the rape,
love was nothing.

A Témpo

Grit to make a pearl
in search of its shell.

The 21st century
coming home to a crying house.

Póco a Póco Dimenuéndo

From the ocean, its mountain:
one fossil star.

In the mass grave
a blue shirt on bones.

Grave

The painter completes
Still Life with Gravel and Opal.

Out comes a swat team
gunning for god.

Fermáta

June and the sonorous bodies
glide in the pool.

Starvation's eye
holding you for the whole note.

Fíne

It's a poem
if it burns like roses.

Antennae rising
here where the stars are wary.

A TYRANNY OF THINGS

—after "Nantucket" by William Carlos Williams

I rubbed the bulbs in mulch and bone meal
till my split cuticles stung
and black hope left its stain
beneath my nails.

See what the dark has rendered:
daffodils, irises nodding their shades
between curtains bleached white,
gleaming with envy

in the afternoon sun. A day is like
glass: hard yet fragile, sharp when broken,
transparent, reflective, useful.
After cleaning

a house full of things, I watch the dust
sift down through shafts of light.
Pitcher, tumbler mean nothing unless
I am thirsty.

Pour me a drink. We will sit
on crisp linen. I will tell you stories
of men who loved things and women
who kept them.

THE GIFT CHILD

*"I give and devise to my son William and to my
grandsons . . . each a negro boy not exceeding
ten years old . . . " –* The Last Will and Testament
of William Cain, written 1827, executed 1834.
(Andrea Tuttle Kornbluh, "William Cain's Will")

I come to you on this day,
the year of your Lord 1834,
not of my own free will
or yours.

       I am the given.
You will receive. What we have in common:
orders we obey without question,
the keeping of others, the dead
father's wish kept alive.

What does this make me?

I will know your nakedness,
help you bathe, help you dress,
cover the shame to which you were born.

I will know your waste and stench,
empty and scour your pots, scrub
the indelicate breach of your body
left on your linens and silks.

I will see your joys but know your tempers,
the fear behind them every moment
rules require I look away,
look away, look away.

What does this make you?

When I look down in your presence,
your legs become the white columns,
your feet their base, your mind
the mansion held up,
held down by them.

Who between us is free?

I will continue to brush the lint
from the shoulders of your gray serge,
though you won't know how to move.

I will continue to fan your sweat to cooling
those August afternoons while you read,
though you won't know how to see.

It is true
I know a lot for my age.
I am only ten, but I have been
here, bought and sold, given and giving
for two-hundred-and-fifteen years.

ENFANT TERRIBLE

After their bodies,
one by sweaty one,
collapse onto mine in the brothel, they walk away
mistaking relief for freedom.

They do not know
they must mother me now.
I have made these men pregnant
with their secret.
I am

the secret
they carry like a nine-pound fetus –
unavoidable
unabortable
never born.

We share the same blood,
same word into image.
We pulse.

I am always
full-term and growing. I roll
and kick, wake them from their sleep
in the bed, on the street,
over dinner with the family,
or while shopping for a new suit.

They need it loose.
They need to let out their belts
to contain me.

Multitudes contain me.
Some will carry me by the dozens.
Some will think
they forget

the sweetness, the light,
the thing they have made:
this new life.

THE POSTMISTRESS

—*for Nellie Woolum (1916-1981)*

I knew it sat high on the ridge above me,
a purse without fare for the journey,
a black eye that never looked down
and yet was weeping.

I knew that they called it a pond
but the algae was gob, the plankton was clay,
and the crawfish and peepers were bony coal.
I knew the water was rock.

I knew how to speak, deliver the story
to bottom lines, bottom lands,
upper hands, bottom lies.
I, a crank without grease.

They told me the wall would hold up
hold up   hold up
                                    hold up
all that was useless to them. Near Christmas

I listened to the rain one night,
let it rock me to sleep, remember being
carried away, hitting a wall, splashing over it.
I sing now. Who listens?

RED LACE

—for Lee Howard

It was not delicate.

It was jagged rock:
sandstone
granite
basalt.

It was not durable.

It graveled away into sand,
gathered into a bar,
split the creek
in two.

It was not warm.

Its ashes looked and felt
like frost.

It was not bright.

You remember looking up,
the full winter moon behind
a grid of limbs.

It was not hand-made
with tenderness.

It was man-made,
hand-held.

It did not come with words.

The silence was mythical:
a swallow, an arrow flying
from and at you.

It was not the trim
around pajamas
or a valentine.

It unraveled
your sleep, your heart,
your book of hours.

It was not sexy.

It was red.

It was not red.

It was blood.

It was not you . . .

. . . and it was.

It would never be beautiful.

A thousand faces.
Not one of them a hero.

It was not a gift
to your economy.

It damned the valley,
then collapsed upon you.

It was everywhere
invisible.

You had to leave Kentucky
to see it, feel it, take it on your own terms,
wrestle it into song.

ASSESSADEMIA

i.
Now I must teach by the grid,
wasting fuel to make thin heat, weak light.

Now I must generate goals and objectives
instead of jack-in-the-pulpits, jack-in-the-boxes, jacks of all trades.

Now I must prove my abilities
the way one might paint Picassos by numbers.

Now I must reach a bottom line
because what's at the bottom serves the top.

ii.
Now I must market my courses to convenience,
my thinking to efficiency, my sense to dollars.

Now I must conceptualize a pedagogy – crinkum-crankum –
and practice professing it works.

Now I must remember that diversity is beautiful
and wonder where it has gone.

Now I must take a pay cut to pay for
the espresso machine in the recently refurbished administration complex.

Now I must watch the grounds of the Corporate University
brew into a bitter cup of *Gotcha by the tits!*

iii.
Now I must say hello to the blossoming technologies
and goodbye to the wilting post-human humanities.

Now I must entertain through a screen
because students must learn to buy more machines.

Now I must teach to images of distant bodies
that are not stars or planets or moons or flesh.

Now I must always be online instead of writing lines.
We are programmed to retrieve.

iv.
Now I must teach a text instead of a tale, a process instead of a
    poem,
and forget that the best stories rise from blood and nerve and
    tactile generosity.

Now I must teach critical thinking
but not criticize the New American Nightmare.

Now I must teach my students:
Beware of your toys.

Now I must learn my not so new names:
Crank, Curmudgeon, Luddite, The Mad Professor.

Now I must somehow find in this job
the good work that answers despair.

V.

A second sea rises . . . .

The Mermaid Parade

See them, one by one, appear
As if the street were one long wave

Hello. To float is to imagine;
They tiptoe on magnificent fins, freed

From the bows of ships, freed
From the inks and paints. Their colors run

Amok with occasional Neptunes.
The pink one with the nail in her tongue

Clicks when she smiles; the white
One splits her smile across two heads. The gold

One with green lips who swallows fire
Grins her black jewels; her partner wears

Long purple fur, manatee manque.
Odd they come in paisleys, plaids, and pinstripes,

Some slick in their polyesters,
Some sinister under mustaches. A radical pause,

And then their queen arrives,
Sequined in newsprint, dripping with tidal

Neglect and current events. She throws
Her mirror down; it shatters into an ocean

Of blue salutes: buildings turn to sand,
Cars and hair have fins again, sharks are still

Sharks, but now we know them
By their tears. The sun drops like an oyster,

The night shucked open for its pearls.
The parade continues to Cleveland, Atlanta, St. Louis,

Missoula, and Boise, stopping just
Shy of California. Nothing can stop them from being

Who they are, but who are we now
With our suitcases full of water, our new

Scales of wonder? Everywhere kelp
And calamity. Everywhere fish out

Of winter. How long can we hold
What their passing has given us:

Imaginary people
With real cities in them?

EVE GATHERING APPLES

Now when I think about it,
now when the fruit still falls from the tree
in lush thuds

and lifting follows the bow
to what has no name without us,
I know

I would never go back.
Never knowing hunger there was a kind
of darkness,

a void no voice
could penetrate, no light open with its flat
rangy hands;

a womb
where reason heard no heartbeat.
So it seemed.

I must have felt
something like hunger the day I said *Why*,
then tasted

fear's gooey tang.
I was not so much driven out as choosing
to pass

through the garden,
through the hinged gate that sang its rust
of good riddance.

Yes, there is
suffering here; sometimes I make it, sometimes
it makes me,

but there was
another breed of suffering in that garden: Beauty
a green perfection

unable to age.
And here's the real curse: you will suffer
to believe it.

Now when I taste
the sweet held crisp beneath the apple's skin,
I swallow

the rot behind it,
not the idea that obedience alone
can save us.

SUPER MODEL

She refuses
to believe

t
h
i
s

i
m
a
g
e

is the best
she can do.

ENLIGHTENED AT EIGHTEEN

I've decided not
to wait for strangers
and other men who
know me from church, school,
and Kroger's as I
walk or cross my legs
or reach for the back
of the top shelf where
the last box of corn
flakes on sale this week
sits against the wall,
so to know if it's
there you have to jump
up and look or first
imagine real hard
to make sure effort
is worth the trouble,
and is it Kellogg's
or the Post Toasties
your Uncle Ed ate
nights watching TV,
or the cheap brand you
think smells like glue but
hunger enough means
who cares what at night —
well, I'm not a box
of corn flakes and that's
the point: I've decided
not to wait for men
and other strangers
to mentally un-
dress me just because
I happen to be

there and they happen
to – uh, well – uh, rise
to my occasion.
I'll make their game my
own and beat them first.
From now on when I
leave the house, I'll go
naked in my mind.
I won't stop at flesh
but strip myself down
to my bones. My ribs
will be their cage. They'll
want to look away
from looking through. My
smile will scare them back
to canned goods, frozen
peas, or deli meats.
I'll leave them starving
for affection. They
won't know where to turn,
the aisles, the sidewalks
where I walk naked
in my mind so long,
so empty. So what
if they still whistle
or snort? Their music
will bounce off my cheek
bones, slap them silly.
Later they'll turn red
with recollection
and I'll be walking,
thinking and singing,
straight up and fleshed out,
my mind apple pie.

THIS LIGHT THIS TIME

What if we were rain
with memory,
could recall

the soulful
and gradual rising,
the gathering into cloud;

the light we carried
as we rose and fell,
this time

along the Appalachians,
drenching the paw-paw,
the hickory, the oak;

drooling into crevices,
becoming the split of stone,
the spit of springs

to come greening the ferns,
sip for the sapsucker
and others

on wing and foot, fin
and root? What if we believed
what the rainbow

of wet gravel
lit through a clear stream
tells us?

What if we were
wings of light
descending

onto peaks forever lost,
onto man&machine-made
songless prairies?

Would our light be
buried in pockets of earth?
Would it   refuse to go out?

Shell of the Moment

It curves,
a gentle S,
a soft wave ever breaking.
Yet small:
you can hold motion in your hand.
If Joan Mitchell worked her pastels
on a pearl canvas, her colors
might shimmer so. Brighter when
wet, when recent.
Pattern you know
you can remember so
you take it, a keeper
filed away in a box full of keepers,
safe, sure to be
forgotten.

No, it whorls,
tunneling deep into itself.
You want to follow yet
know you've been there,
are coming out of it, really,
into open   everywhere
opening.
              Sometimes abandoned,
carried off by another. *Theft*
the word you use for your care-
lessness.
Apex to aperture
every step has built its wall
between you and beginning.
Only a curve in the future
can hollow you back.

No, it breaks
in half.
Muscles that scuttled shut
and open long
gone into something else.
The borings: anything fine
can sift right through,
even the light
if held so.
                Anchor for other
attachments now
abandoned. But the links
remain: layered white
tubing of worms surpass the edge,
pipes from an organ no
longer playing. But look
hard enough: you can imagine
the music in
your hands.

No, it fractures,
noun become verb. No one
event or eruption, no blood-
stained epiphany. Instead
a constant gentle pounding,
music resolute
you sing to,
surfacing.
You lose sight of individuals
unless you stoop to the scale
of sand: colors, ridges,
edges emerge; shapes
soften into other shapes, sounds
disclosing.

Going here.
How good it feels beneath your feet:
a standing   a sinking
                    at once.

No, it precedes you:
older, harder,
heavier than you remembered,
filled with substance made
familiar by its lack of distinction;
or does the occasional crystal jut
forth, lone tooth of the last
bite for air?
You know the science: what is
preserved is still
changed,
here and away at once. Is
why you find beauty
when it takes the sick gray
that stone can wear:
you still
feel its ridges in your palm
when the next moment comes
to collect you,
and the next, wave
after gentle wave,
pounding.

MEDITATION AT USELESS BAY

At neap tide I walk the low
range of beach at Useless Bay

and Double Bluff, gaze from water
to rock-studded glacial sands

pricked with gorse and grasses.
They waver and grip.

I collect the patience
of starfish and sea urchins

succulent in their pools,
cannot resist the cobbles,

abandoned moon shells
and barnacles. Keepsakes,

triggers to fire me back
to cold salts of the past,

to make time
as hard a thing as place.

On a small dune up
from the wash zone, I find

a thumb-nail disk of sandstone,
fragile fractal of the bluff.

Weathered rock waste is what
the book will call it, remnants

cemented and compressed
by the old, glue-factory earth,

made further by erosion,
surviving its own making

to arrive in my hands.
This gritty disk of stone,

this time. Should I keep it
like the others, break the cycle

however briefly, save it
from nothing a while longer?

Later I will hear a sifting sound,
then a trickling, watch

a pockety-floosh of sand and rock
cascade down the bluff,

piling fresh and dark,
fluvial and traceable

up to the spooned-out
slope beneath the ridge

where eagles cry out, drift,
and settle again.

SLUG TIME ON WHIDBEY ISLAND

Glistening a young banana slug
has come to the end
of its hemlock.

Its tentacled eyes and head slowly
scoop through the air,
a yellow spoon

that stops me. I am learning
how the shift into
slug time

can quicken my thoughts. I wait,
watch the juvenile make
a mid-air u-turn,

head back up the soft-needled limb
and disappear to later,
perhaps,

descend on a silver thread of its slime
to the forest floor,
feed on lichen,

mushrooms, algae, poison oak,
droppings and decay,
avoiding shrews

and beetles, to be the poet it is,
breaking down what
passes in life

to help this garden, this earth,
give back again
in kind.

Epilogue

MARRELLA IN THE SANDS

I.

Sea nymph on a node of time, beached
at last on Cambrian's rocky shore.

Charles Walcott split the rock to clear a path.
You reappeared: a film of carbon gleaming.

He sketched your stains of being: lace of gills,
spines like tusks; torso, legs, antennae.

Many have climbed the mountain to reach you,
measuring distance in hundreds of millions of years.

Alien, orphan, prodigal among our kingdoms:
names and families divide us, yet this our reef.

II.

Drifting above the mud-drenched sands,
did you sense the twisting heights to come?

Deposit-feeder, filtering sustenance out of sludge.
We have no sacred text as deep as your life.

All of us more than shadow, substance, fluke;
all of these, but more is the blank we fill with longing.

Many have pulled you from cabinets and shelves,
your presence a poem that walks in our sleep.

X-rayed, peeled apart, drawn and quartered.
We picture you to see where – what – we are.

III.
Like you we once were blind, less
than an inch long, drifting in a temporary sea.

You lived with many along an algal reef
as fragile and surprising as our beginnings.

I walk down my street and think of your body
shaped like antennae disappearing from roof-tops.

Norm and anomaly: something to tell us.
What dying star lent you its chemistry?

You: a word, a letter in small black print,
a lasting song sung less than *soto voce*.

IV.
Ego arrhythmic in the wake of your seasons;
no seascape close enough for these dry hours.

Like many I gather your descendants by the fistfuls,
hard little whispers that trouble the noise.

Do I find in you a lost piece of myself
or is it your mystery that sings me awake?

Perhaps we collect to slap back the hand of time,
to keep from getting snatched ourselves.

Art, artifact, fossil: traveler in the stone,
you beckon us now to move.

NOTES

Sources for phrases and excerpts used as section titles are as follows:

Section I, "Wave Train," *Encyclopedia Britannica* online, acc.
    May 23, 2016.
Section II, Henry Beston, *The Outermost House*, 1928; rpt. 1992,
    p. 43.
Section III, William J. Neal et al., *Atlantic Coast Beaches*, 2009,
    Mountain Press, p. 60.
Section IV, Rachel Carson, *The Sea Around Us*, 1950; rpt. 1989,
    Oxford University Press, p. 114.

Dreaming Out of Deep Time: The italicized comments in part
II are excerpts from online reviews of the Fossil Motel in Fossil,
Oregon.

Now and Then: The significance of "empty hands" is borrowed
from "Provision" by W. S. Merwin.

The Transposition Blues: The line "creeping toward the news" is
a variation of a phrase from Theodore Roethke's *Straw for the Fire*.

The Postmistress: Nellie Woolum, a retired postmistress in Ages
(Harlan County), Kentucky, was killed when a coal refuse pond
above her house collapsed. The pond was owned by Eastover
Mining.

Red Lace: Lee Howard's work is collected in *Harvest of Fire*,
edited by George Ella Lyon.

***Marrella* in the Sands**: *Marrella splendens* is a fossil arthro-
pod, part of the Cambrian radiation, first discovered by Charles
Doolittle Walcott, in 1909, in the Burgess shale of the Canadian
Rockies.

ABOUT THE AUTHOR

RHONDA PETTIT is a member of the Southern Appalachian Writers Cooperative, and the author of *Fetal Waters* (a poetry chapbook published by Finishing Line Press, 2012), and *The Global Lovers* (a poetic drama produced at the 2010 Cincinnati Fringe Festival). Two of her poems and an essay have been nominated for a Pushcart Prize. She teaches creative writing and literature at the University of Cincinnati Blue Ash College, where she is editor of the *Blue Ash Review*, hosts and co-produces *The Poetry Café* for UCTV Online, and conducts a poetry festival annually. Her individual and collaborative collages and poetry (with H. Michael Sanders) were included in three exhibitions and their related print and online publications: *Gaps & Overlaps, Dada Lives!,* and at the *Faculty and Staff Art Exhibition* at the UCBA Art Gallery in 2015, 2016, and 2017. Her scholarship on the work of Dorothy Parker produced two books, *A Gendered Collision* (2000) and *The Critical Waltz* (2005). She also served as one of the poetry editors for both volumes of *The Aunt Lute Anthology of U.S. Women Writers* (Hogeland et al., 2004 and 2008).

Author photo by Pete Bender.

FOR THE FULL DOS MADRES PRESS CATALOG:
www.dosmadres.com